Best wishes

Do You Remember?

For those who 'care' to remember

Ted Dakin

by Ted Dakin

Ted Dakin

Ted Dakin grew up in a world of poverty, with a poor education at a tough Catholic school. But the world he lived in was full of interesting people and amusing goings on, and he based his many nostalgic stories on these characters and his upbringing. This booklet, however, is more down to earth and his meant to give hope, confidence and mental stimulation by reminding our ever increasing aged population of the past and to bring back the good memories of a time that is fast disappearing.

Contents

Do You Remember Wigan Wakes Week? *5*

Do You Remember Coping With Illness? *5*

Do You Remember Family Life? *7*

Do You Remember Life Before The Demolition Men? *10*

The Power Of No! *12*

Food, Glorious Food *14*

A Golden Age *16*

"I'm Cowder Than Mon In T'Park" *19*

'Shop Till You Drop' *21*

"You're Nicked!" *22*

DO YOU REMEMBER WIGAN WAKES WEEK?

For the first week of every July, the noise and hustle and bustle of Wigan's cotton mills fell silent. Other industries too, either closed their doors or kept going with a reduced workforce. Even a few shops put up their shutters.

And where did these hard-working folk go on holiday? You guessed it. Blackpool, Southport, Rhyl, Llandudno, and various other resorts, were invaded by hopeful, sun-seeking, fun-loving, thirsty and hungry holiday-makers that were the town's working classes. They travelled by steam train, bus or charabanc. If you stayed at home, the town was deserted and boredom set in, so, to break the monotony, you booked a day trip by charabanc. The coach firms of Smiths, Barnes, and other companies did a roaring trade. Those well-upholstered, but cramped single-deckers, took a route that included a stop at some tiny rural cafe – there were no motorways in those days – then off again to the seaside resorts of Wales or to Scarborough or Morecambe, and of course the favourite one of all, Blackpool; and there was one thing for sure, wherever you went, you were certain to bump into someone you knew; workmates, neighbours, and distant relatives, even your boss.

"How do, Joe, where et stoppin'?"

"Well, if it isn't our Sammy... how long art 'ere fer?"

"Hello, Molly, luv, ha thowt thee an' Billy were gooin to New Brighton."

All good friends out to have a good time. Then the hunt for a good fish and chip shop, followed by a paddle in the sea, before tea.

DO YOU REMEMBER COPING WITH ILLNESS?

I remember as a lad, and I don't know why, it always seemed to be a dark, cold winter's night – when a bowler-hatted Mr. Harmer, doctor Berry's man, came calling every Friday about six o'clock to collect six pence ($2^{1/2}$p in today's money) to cover the whole family for minor medical problems. There wasn't any NHS in those days.

And I also remember Dad and me during the hot Summer months, walking down the canal bank to gather herbs. Plants such as dandelion and burdock and nettle, from which Dad made dandelion and burdock (non-alcoholic) beer. When it was brewed it had the appearance of today's lager beer; and believe me, it was nectar in a bottle.

And everyone knows the cure for nettle stings; rub a dock leaf on the affected part, and hey presto! The sting disappears. Isn't it strange, the dock plant is always found in close proximity to stinging nettle? Back in olden times, country folk reckoned that the dock leaf was most effective if the following spell was said simultaneously. *"NETTLE OUT, DOCK IN- DOCK REMOVE THE NETTLE'S STING"*

True or not, it gives the whole idea of herbs and folklore a certain charm and quaintness. Dad and I also gathered comfrey, which has several common names – the most popular one being, knitbone. Dad would hang the leaves and allow them to dry, and when anyone suffered a strain, bruise or swelling, he would put the leaves in a pan of water and simmer them for about 20 minutes, then the victim would bathe the injured part until relief was obtained.

But in those days, even if you didn't know your herbs, there was always a herbalist shop within easy walking distance, where you could buy, for a few coppers, any herb, for any complaint under the sun; all nature's remedies, which, with a bit of knowledge, could be gathered personally from local fields and meadows

And do you remember too, friendly neighbours nipping next door to make cinder tea for a new born baby with the gripes? When money was short, which was often, they couldn't afford gripe water, so they made cinder tea. And this is how it was done:

Take a red-hot cinder out o't fire, put it in a cup of cold water, let it stand for a few seconds, put in some sugar, let it stand some more, sieve it into another cup, let it cool again, then pour it into the babies bottle. That got the wind-up, I'll tell you!

So, if you fancy reviving an age-old remedy for the gripes, why not have a go? And if you can do this with a modern gas fire, write it down, get it published, and you'll make a fortune.

Now, the humble potato, as everyone knows, is not an herb, but a vegetable. But it was once believed that a stolen potato was a useful charm against rheumatism, and would be carried in a pocket or around the neck.

And warts rubbed with a potato would disappear as the vegetable rotted. Personally, I like my spuds on a plate, chipped, boiled or mashed, or made into a belly-filling hash.

And while we are on the subject of beliefs and the mysterious folklore of plants; the leek, the national emblem of Wales, was once regarded as a young lady's means of meeting her future husband. By walking backwards into a garden and placing a knife amongst a row of leeks, she would see a vision of her future beloved.

DO YOU REMEMBER FAMILY LIFE?

Do you remember when you were growing up? How can you ever forget? Especially, if like me, you were brought up in the depression years; when the dole queues were long and money was scarce. I honestly think that when life is hard it leaves you with an indelible memory of the times endured. Not that you resented those times and conditions. How could you? You didn't know any different. Take the example of our house where I, my two brothers, and sister were born and raised.

Ours, like many more, had one cold water tap and a shallow brown 'slop stone'. Until we could afford a geyser, our only means of obtaining hot water was by boiling the kettle. Yes, we had a boiler, a copper one inside a brick surround, with room for a small coal fire underneath. It was situated in a corner near the back kitchen window, and on washdays, Mam would make a fire, pile in the dirty clothes and boil them, using a stick to stir the clothes around. Afterwards, the clothes were scrubbed and squeezed through a mangle. That was one of my jobs after school, turning the mangle for Mam.

When Dad was out of work, Mam took in washing to make an extra bob or two. It wasn't a nice job, not in those days, anyway. And what about the toilet set up? Our lavvy was a good 50 yards up the communal backyard. That meant at night we had to use a chamber pot. Everyone had a 'po' under the bed. And those bedrooms were colder than a butcher's fridge. It didn't make things any better having to hop across the cold linoleum and down uncarpeted stairs, either. Coal was kept under the stairs, and as well as heating the copper boiler, it was our only means of heating the living-room, and that is where Mam did her cooking and baking, on a black-leaded, fire range. On some winter's nights I actually looked forward to spending time in front of the fire, pegging a rug made from sacking and pieces of coloured, unwanted clothing, like jackets and trousers. That same fire heated the solid (no wire in those days) plate oven shelves, which Mam, on a cold winter's night, wrapped in a blanket to warm our beds. An unforgettable luxury.

We never had much money, but Dad worked hard – when he was in work – and Mam, scraped, saved, baked and slaved, to give us the best of what was on offer.

When coal was in short supply, which was often, me and Dad

would push Grandad's wheelbarrow to the gasworks in Sovereign Road, fill a couple of sacks with coke, and trundle them back home. They cost a shilling a bag, if I remember rightly. Now, coke was a devil to stoke up, so you needed a few pieces of wood, a few lumps of coal (if you were lucky enough to have any) a shovel, a sheet of the Wigan Observer, placed against the fireplace, and away it went. But it still required plenty of attention.

Every year, when winter arrived, (and they were gradely winters too) and you lived like us in the bottom house in Miry Lane, those icy winds would howl down the canal bank, past Gallagher's bone works and whistle through those generous window-gaps, up skirts and trouser legs, threatening to amputate certain parts of one's anatomy. Those gaps were that wide, you could pop your hand through and wave to a passing neighbour. And that's the truth... well, nearly. Over the winter months, oil-lamps, even candles in jars and bottles, were placed close to lavatories' water pipes to prevent a burst or freeze-up. If you were unlucky enough to have a burst – and with the landlady working on the assumption that a burst would only occur again if repaired, she left well alone and you had to carry water from house to lavvy until better weather arrived. Rolled-up newspapers' shoved in the window-gaps served as our central heating, but, Miss Ballard, the landlady, still called for the weekly rent of four shillings and sixpence, which was always enforced with a regular quote "Halfpennies make pennies, pennies make shillings and shillings make pounds". Then, the cheeky so-and-so would pocket the money, and initial the rent book before skipping off to another 'undesirable residence' round the corner.

How on earth did we ever manage in those early years of austerity? No TV, toasters, telephones, Hoovers, central heating or double glazing. No carpeted bedrooms or stairs or electric lights. A sparsely carpeted living-room, with a solid square dinner table in the middle and one gas mantle above it. And God help anyone who broke a precious gas mantle!

There was one luxury though (apart from the black-leaded fire range, of course). And that was our acid battery wireless in the corner. A miracle of modern invention. And, towering above all this, Mam and Dad: unflappable, strong and reliable. Especially Mam; she ran our home with love discipline and tact.

Deep in the cobwebs of my mind, I can still hear her voice echoing up our rickety stairs and into the bedroom

"Edward, Edward, are you out of bed yet? You're going to be late for school." I knew if I lingered much longer it would mean a cold wet flannel across my face.

But that was life. A two up and two down terraced house, landlord owned. But we called it *"OUR HOUSE" DO YOU REMEMBER?*

DO YOU REMEMBER LIFE BEFORE THE DEMOLITION MEN?

I do. That was a time before whole communities had to move out.

I was born and bred in a part of Wigan where trust, compassion and camaraderie, went hand in hand, when a knock on a neighbour's door didn't warrant an answer, a lift of the latch, a cheery hello, a cup of tea and a good natter, was an everyday occurrence.

Where did they go, these friends and neighbours? They went to unfamiliar surroundings, amongst people they didn't know. Some went to council bungalows, some to high-rise flats, and took their memories with them, to remember carefree Sunday jaunts along the canal to Gathurst, armed to the teeth with jam butties and bottles of tap water – I can still see those breadcrumbs floating around in those bottles. Then the walk home, sun-tanned, tired, but happy, starving hungry; to be greeted with the mouth-watering aromas of Mam's scrumptious home-made bread, cakes and pies, and of course, custard, blancmange and jelly. And, after tea, back outside playing street games till dusk, followed by a thorough scrub-down at the slop-stone, then up the 'wooden hill' to bed.

How can you ever forget where you were born and bred? Where neighbours loved, cried, laughed, married and died. I remember a certain Mrs. Clark who lived a few doors from us, who was the proud owner of a pedal-type organ. God only knows where she got it from, but she would often entertain many a passer-by by belting out those popular tunes of the day: *WHEN POPPIES BLOOM AGAIN... IT'S ONLY A SHANTY IN OLD SHANTY TOWN...* and so on. When they decided to get rid of it, they discovered that it wouldn't go through the front door and it took 2 days to dismantle the instrument!

Every area had their own 'fortune teller' – tea leaf readers, palm readers, all of them giving hope to those who believed in them. Local legend had it that one of these ladies predicted that one neighbour's husband would lose a leg.

Later, because his wife was poorly, he did the shopping, bought a leg of lamb, called for a pint and left it in the snug. He never did get that leg back!

Then there was Jack 'Pegleg' Southworth and his little wife, Harriet. Jack had a pirate-type wooden leg, which, along with his front door, he tarred twice a year in order to preserve them. They only possessed a hearth rug, so Harriet would apply a rubbing stone to their living-room floor as well as her front step, until they both shone like alabaster.

Oddly enough there were plenty of pubs in those days. Our local, The Crown Inn, had regular Saturday night sing-songs with Paddy on the piano, Harry, tenor solo (well sort of) and Mavis, soprano. Then there was my mate, Billy, the finest accordionist for miles around. Every Saturday night, I (his best friend) played an important role in this world of entertainment. Between satisfying slurps of complimentary beer, I would (strenuously) turn the pages of his music sheets, while Billy, down to his shirt sleeves and with tie undone, rattled out the tunes everyone knew. 'Danny Boy', 'Just a Song at Twilight' 'Bless this House' and many more. When time was called, it was out on the street, a call for fish and chips, followed by raucous street singing, then home to bed. What a night!

These were the hard times of 'make-do-and-mend' Nothing was thrown away unless it was completely useless. Clothes were worn to the extreme, and always neatly patched and sewn to extend wear and handed down to the next in line. Even then, the better parts were used to make a 'pegged' rug for the living-room hearth. If you were lucky enough to wear something new like shoes or a jacket, there was always a flippant remark to contend with.

"What shop did thy break into, mate?"

Or if it was something ill-fitting or didn't suit them.

"Look at 'er, shop must 'ave been giving them away free."

All said without malice or intent; at a time when folk wanted things they just could not afford, but didn't give a damn, and got on with living best way they could.

How times (and people) have changed. Or should that be, how times have changed people?

I don't mean in a technological sense. Although, even in our advanced technological world, there haven't been any Utopian benefits, that's for sure; and technology hasn't made us a better-living race of people.

Along the rocky road of progress we seem to have lost the art of living together. Some customs and conventions have suffered dramatically. People don't care much for other people anymore. We are utterly swamped in a morass of self-indulgence, where a plastic card will buy you what you want, and beggar the consequences.

THE POWER OF NO!

Apart from the various connotation of the word NO! It is only when used in the in the context of denial or refusal, that it becomes most powerful; and often, the most hated. But should it be used more often as a word for discipline? Have we lost, or forgotten, the advantages of saying *NO*? Surely, the demands of today's children for possessions, wealth, and fame could be better monitored if parents (and grandparents) made better use of that word and its true meaning. Is there a link between its lack of use and the inevitable rise and rise of violence, cruelty and dishonour? Is the lack of use turning some children into monsters? Are we, as elders and guardians, so willing to please and placate the young ones? If so, would using that word more often, make our children (and their children, too) more sociable and compassionate?

Were they better times when money was scarce? When empty purses and dented money boxes were scrutinized and fretted over? When we didn't know which way to turn, when buying one thing meant not buying another. When children who often heard the word *NO*! ran off to play, and ask another day.

Gone are the days when the word of a parent was law and was accepted as such. Kids were kids and tantrums were thrown, but house rules were abided by. It was usually left to Mother to lay down the law, and Dad, sitting in his fireside chair, buried his head into his newspaper and said nowt. Unless, of course, a firmer, more threatening attitude was called for.

Back then, in penurious times, before plastic money and ISAs and loans and omnipresent cars and televisions, people lived within their means. They had their wants, but they were necessary wants; when the choice was perhaps a pair of shoes or a Sunday roast, and an old tea caddy held the household savings, which the kids knew about, but never opened. It was a time when Dad, who happened to have a few coppers left over from his 'pocket money' handed it back to his grateful 'bank manager'... his wife.

A wife who knitted, sewed, darned, crocheted, and worried, and said *NO*! to her ever demanding family, who knew that word so well, and heard it so often, accepted it, because she was the boss.

So, are modern parents as strong as they should be? Would our children be better children and less demanding if they heard and respected that small, but powerful word... *NO*! more often?

"Can I go out?"

"*NO*!"

"Can I watch tele?"

"*NO*!"

Can I have this, that and t'other. *NO*! *NO*! *NO*! Just imagine the impact.

And there's something else about the word *NO*! It gives the enforcer of that word a feeling of doing good, of doing right.

And would we be a happier, slimmer race of people if we all said *NO*! more often?

It could even help control the world's ever increasing population. Well, maybe, maybe not, but the advantages are limitless.

FOOD, GLORIOUS FOOD

Do you remember those bygone days when dietitian was just a word in the dictionary? Today, it's not just a word, in its plural form, it means an army of dietary killjoys, bombarding us with advice on what and what not to eat, and even when to eat it. They tell us what's good for us, what's bad for us, watch our intake of sugar, salt and fat. Check this. Check that. And on and on it goes.

It's no wonder people are confused and bewildered by this continual attack of do's and don'ts. Even our most basic of foodstuff is now viewed with suspicion. This advisory body of busybodies has taken the pleasure out of eating. They've taken over our lives and robbed us of the ability to choose for ourselves. They do our thinking for us, but it hasn't always been like this.

Do you remember the days before the rise and rise of these dietitians? We, the working-classes – the poor folk – even in those penniless times of want, always tried to keep a 'good' table. Not necessarily a balanced diet, but a good table, all the same. Good thick broths made with plenty of veg and left to simmer for ages in a pot that included a good sized bone from the butchers, 'just to give it plenty o' body', and then mopped up with chunks of Mam's home-made white bread. By, 'eck, just the thought makes me drool. And what about those home-made steak and kidney puddings? Bursting with meat and gravy that made you dizzy with anticipa-tion. And there was always plenty of spuds. The ubiquitous potato. How can you survive without potatoes? As previously mentioned, boiled, chipped, mashed or made into a belly-filling hash. All followed with plenty of rice pudding or Mam's currant cake smothered in butter. And what about those thick dripping butties! All good body sustaining food, containing enough stodge – which they now tell us not to eat – to block your arteries just by looking at it. Lovely!

We knew plenty o' fat folk, too, and thin; but we didn't make comparisons. There were just fat folk, thin folk, and in between folk; and that was it.

There were no keep-fit clubs or dietitians, we just got on with living and being ourselves. Our main exercise was walking. To the shops, to work, to the cinema, pubs and clubs. Did they have taxi-cabs in those days? Even our leisure time was spent walking. Haigh Hall, Wigan Park, along the canal towpath. If you saw someone running and in a sweat, you knew he'd done something wrong.

The cobbler's shops in those days did a roaring trade, repairing shoes and clogs was a lucrative trade. They did a good job too. Thick leather for shoes, and strong irons for clogs.

I remember my Dad too – to save a few bob – renewing the irons on our clogs, and repairing our shoes. I can still smell the aroma of new leather and cobbler's wax, all poignant reminders of a working-class past.

Those were the days when no one, with the exception of sick folk dieted. Your Mam cooked the grub, put it on the table and you scoffed the lot. So, no keep-fit classes, but instead everyone took a walk to somewhere.

Do you remember how many picture houses there were in Wigan's town centre? If, like me, you spent more time visiting these palatial places of entertainment than you did visiting relatives, then you'll remember right enough.

They've all gone now. But the memories linger on. Memories of a golden age of entertainment. Do you remember the Ritz in Station Road? (even the road has vanished). This was Wigan's most stylish cinema. It was at this cinema that I first saw The Adventures of Robin Hood, with the dashing Errol Flynn as Robin. I think it was 1938, the same year the film was released.

Just short walk from the Ritz, tucked away up a narrow passageway just of Marketplace was the Empire, I think this was the smallest picture house in town, and if my memory serves me right, if you wanted a seat in the 'gods' (a balcony seat) you had to climb up a iron fire escape on the side of the building. I wonder what our present day health and safety brigade would have to say about that? Another short stroll from where a policeman used 'direct traffic' and then down Wallgate to the Clarence Hotel, where at the rear, was the Princes cinema (now a night club).

If you walked under Wallgate Bridge for a few hundred yards, and then just past Clayton Street, you would reach Wallgate cinema, but we used to call it 'The Scratch' because after every visit to this establishment you were certain to come out itching like mad. The proprietress, a huge woman with peroxide hair, doled out used comics such as the Beano, Dandy and Hotspur, after you'd collected your admission ticket. Back up Wallgate again, turn right into King Street and on to the County Playhouse, a building that still displays, high above the entrance, the date it was built, 1916. Although now another night club, I think it was this cinema that first introduced a back row of double seats for courting couples.

A few yards down, on the opposite side was the Royal Court Theatre (the 'court') to us Wigan peasants (and which is yet another night club). The one exceptional treat for the patrons of this cinema, was the electronic organ (played by a one-legged organist) that would rise majestically a few feet as he played some favourite tunes, before and during the interval. Cross the road again, to what used to be Lewis's milk bar, and onwards to the Hippodrome, which, until it burnt down in 1956, was Wigan's one and only music-hall, where acts of every type appeared on the bill. Singers, dancers, acrobats, magicians and actors performed to a mesmerised audience. I remember seeing Sweeny Todd, the Demon Barber of Fleet Street, played with such an amusing twist, my ribs ached with laughter. I also recall the Shakespeare Hotel next door, each of its walls adorned with signed photographs of every artist who had appeared at the Hippodrome. I often wonder where those photographs ended up, because they would certainly stir many a happy memory of those bygone days. Just a few strides down from the 'Hipp' was the Palace cinema. As I recollect, its first entrance was like a wide entry with a sloping 'walkway' that was divided by a brown painted wooden handrail.

The walkway took you to the booking office, and admission tickets for the downstairs front stalls (the pit) and the back stalls. The walkway on the left was used as the exit. To purchase tickets for the balcony (the gods) you went past the sloping walkways to the main entrance at the top of some marble steps. These tickets were more expensive, but I always preferred a balcony seat, because down below I was always unlucky enough to be seated behind a chap with a big head or woman with a mop of hair like a busby. While we're at the Palace, I remember a male, effeminate, usher, who roamed the aisles with a torch that would have put a wartime searchlight to shame, and when spotting some unfortunate couple in a passionate clinch, would shout out, loud and clear:

"And you can cut that out, you mucky devils, or I'll have you thrown out!"

Just around the corner from the Palace, at the bottom of

Library Street, was the Pavilion Picturedrome. Who can ever forget that splendid ornamental frontage of the 'Pav' as we used to call it? Now the Pavilion was one place where I would definitely take my chances in a downstairs seat with the big heads and the busbys, because upstairs – the gods – which was always referred to as 'The Monkey Rack' was the place to avoid if you wanted to relax and enjoy the picture; because up there, there was more goings-on (monkey business) than an overcrowded zoo in the mating season.

But our world of entertainment, the silver screens, those clean (with the odd exception) and comfortable cinemas, that could seat hundreds, was slowly, irrevocably strangled to death by the technological advance of a square box in the corner of everyone's living-room. Television! A box that round the clock spews out so much rubbish, with deplorable plots, and dialogue, containing streams of obscenities, so that your finger hovers over the channel-changing button, like a sniper with his finger on the trigger. Even so, I concede that there is some outstanding TV material made specifically for the small screen. Adaptations from classic novels and suchlike, and even shows from the silver screen era. All good stuff. But, reliability and consistency just isn't there. Back in the days I am referring to, we lived in a world when Hollywood was part of that world, when American film stars reigned like royalty. Bogart, Flynn, Fonda, Gable and Tracy. Marlene Dietrich, Bette Davis, Joan Crawford, and a whole lot more. And the British too, flew the flag, with talent and films that proved to the rest of the world, that we were up there with the best.

Aye, along King Street alone, you could enter another world, a world of drama, humour, romance, cowboys and Indians, song and dance. Now what do we have? King Street is now 'binge street' where you can get legless until dawn, stagger outside, regurgitate your 'happy hour' booze, go into another club across the way and start again.

Saturday night and Sunday morning on the town, eh! Who would have thought that a whole way of life like the one we once knew would disappear forever?

Are we living in a lost world? Coalmines, gone! Communities, gone! Corner shops, gone! Cotton mills, gone! Decent, law-abiding pubs, gone! Cinemas, gone! An essential part of life that was Englishness, which made us a nation apart, and one to be proud of, gone!

Aye, they've taken it all, but the memories of us owd 'uns live on. Binge Street will always be King Street, the picture houses will always be remembered, and while there are still some us around, they will live on, and on, until the memories are no more.

"I'M COWDER THAN MON IN T'PARK"

Can you remember when you heard that familiar, old Wigan saying? Meaning, of course, the seated figure of Sir Francis Sharp Powell, MP and Baronet.

I say it on a regular basis, because I'm one those unfortunate characters with 'thin blood'. I'm always cowd; hands, feet, face, and body, the lot! But I don't moan about it... Well, not much, but I'll tell you what, do you remember the winter of 2009-10 (the coldest for three decades, or so they tell us) really tested me, and I must admit, I did my share of complaining. But what a carry on with the media. TV, radio, and newspapers, latched on to those atrocious conditions like it had never happened before. The weather had more coverage than World War Two. What with those never ending, dismal weather reports coming at us from all sides, *and* the recession, I felt like topping myself. I thought, why carry on? Freezing to death and not much money to cheer me up, where will it all end?

Then I began to remember. I began to think back to the winters of times gone by. And every winter was the same. Feet deep snowfalls that temporarily changed the character of our towns, cities and countryside (not flakes of snow floating down to earth like moon dust). We endured frost that lasted for weeks on end, its iron-like grip fracturing pipes and transforming our miserable houses into bricks and mortar fridges, with one coal fire struggling in vain to keep us warm.

As an employee of the newly-formed Makerfield Water Board, I remember especially, the winter of 1962-63. It was certainly the most damaging that I've ever experienced and it lasted for 3 long months without a let-up. The cold was so severe that frost went into the ground to a depth of 2 feet or more, and was responsible for countless underground burst mains and services, which left in their wake collapsed roads and flooded houses. As soon as one burst main was repaired, another popped up further along the road. A record of 12 burst mains in one day occurred in Hindley alone.

Aye, it was a bad un, and we, like everyone else, skidded, cursed and struggled our way through, and never thought once about giving up. Nevertheless, although my working days are long gone, I don't want to experience another winter like 1962-63. So, I've been doing some deep thinking. Early on, before winter sets in, I'm going to visit that mon in t'park, I can see him now, chin resting on the thumb of his right hand and that steady, thoughtful gaze looking down at me; then I'm going to give that shiny shoe of his a vigorous rub and make a wish, and that wish will be for a mild winter; because, you see, I don't want to steal the man's reputation. I don't want to be cowder than him. I don't want folk passing me in t' street and nudging one another and saying.

"Look at 'im... he looks cowder than that mon in t' park."

Anyway, who knows what the future will bring? I mean, what will happen when full scale global warming arrives, will his reputation go up in smoke? (so to speak). Personally, I don't think so. I think us Wigan folk will always be shivering and blowing on our digits in the middle of winter, cursing like hell and saying: *"I'M COWDER THAN THAT MON IN T' PARK"*

'SHOP TILL YOU DROP'

Can anyone remember when it all began? How and when did men become womanised? Even the uneducated know (or should know) that our distant ancestors were responsible for 'bringing home the bacon'. Way back then, while the womenfolk pottered around their stony caves and reared unwashed kids, our intrepid male relatives, armed with just a club or makeshift spear, and wearing his 'second-hand' itchy hairy suit that once belonged to some wild, ferocious animal, would – with great reluctance, I suppose – set forth on what could have been a 'shop till you drop' extreme, shopping expedition. Away he goes, to seek out, kill and carve-up a few months supply of a once menacing, wild beast, so that he and his family could survive the rigours of a cold, cave-dwelling existence. But that was many moons ago. How times have changed. How did it all come about? Can you remember?

Two World Wars brought out the best in our female counterparts and, inevitably, changed their outlook on life forever. But did they, the female species, with their new-found strength, abilities and authority, cast a spell on their domineering spouses? It's hard to say. But it happened. Somewhere along the way, woman, the shopper, head cook and bottle-washer, cleaner and all-round human dynamo, has surrendered her pedestal. Somewhere in the hazy past, men have taken control of what was once an exclusive female role, and because of this mysterious change, men have become womanized. It certainly didn't happen in the 1930's, 40's or 50's.

Back then, to see a man carrying a shopping basket would have been a ludicrous, eye-popping sight, indeed. Just imagine bumping into a craggy-faced coal miner carrying a basket and mingling with a gaggle of chattering housewives in corner shops, fish and chip shops and local chemists! The mind boggles. Those were the days when man, the master of his castle, didn't even fill a kettle. Nope, brewing tea, cooking meals and cleaning was definitely a woman's job and macho-man was happy to sit back and watch, sit down and eat, and then sit back again, replete and contented in his comfy fireside chair before falling asleep, while his wife cleared the table and washed the pots, after which she would pick up her knitting and carry on with her husband's cable stitch cardigan.

But I ask once again, do you remember what brought on this change? Even if a man's wife had died there was always a woman – a relative, or a good-natured neighbour, ready to step in and 'do' for him. To wash his clothes and clean and shop. The only time a man went shopping was when he was out of fags. Now what do we have? The womanized man. We clean – well, sort of. We cook (have you watched television lately?) and we go out and shop. My God! It just doesn't seem right, jostling with women along supermarket aisles and in town centre shops, I mean, just think back to your childhood. Girls played at 'keeping house' and serving tea, and boys played at 'Dad' and cowboys and Indians, and that was it! The great divide. And that's how it should be. But it's too late I'm afraid. The rot has set in. Gone for always are the days when we hirsute hunters left our stone-littered caves and set forth with spear and club, to do our very own ultimate 'shop till you drop' trip, and with not one shopping bag or woman in sight.

"YOU'RE NICKED!"

Do you remember when every decent law-abiding citizen could walk our streets, day or night, in dark or light, without fear? Now we live in disturbing times of yobs, happy slappers, muggers and predators, who prey on honest, law abiding townsfolk. Times have changed drastically. Daily, we are constantly given details of violent crimes. Muggings, rapes, and murder are on the increase. And, although shocked and disturbed, we have come to accept these atrocities. In what was once a better age, violence of any kind was more upsetting. It was discussed, analysed and fretted over in detail. Now, it's taken for granted. Back then the criminal paid the penalty befitting the crime and justice was done.

Do you remember when there seemed to be bobbies everywhere? Walking their beats, directing traffic, directing lost old ladies and passing the time of day. Now, they are motorized, zooming past in police cars. Today, meeting a pedestrian policeman is a wonder to behold. It's no wonder criminals have lost their fear of being literally caught red-handed. Yobs, hooligans, louts and burglars seem to be winning. They have no fear. Fear of capture, of being apprehended, was at one time (and still should be) a deterrent.

Gone are the days when you could leave your front door unlocked, bicycles left out and unchained, purses left on sideboards and tables. But not any more. This was a time of honour and respect. Respect for people and property.

Could it be that (apart from more policing, of course) more discipline in the home is the answer to certain acts of lawlessness?

Back in better times, discipline and the act of caring went hand in hand. Neighbours cared for the sick and infirmed. In times of trouble there was strong, dependent shoulders to lean on.

Neighbours gave help to those worse off than themselves, and they didn't expect anything in return, not even a thank-you. That's how it was in those days. And do you remember, everyone 'Honoured their Father and their Mother'. But if you did wrong, you were severely disciplined, just the same.

Mam was the lawgiver in our house, and ruled with a firm, care-worn hand, which, when the occasion arose, gave a gradely, well-aimed clout across the lughole. And what about discipline in the classroom? Today, the liberal thinkers recommend leniency, which has left some teachers confused and powerless. But as some of us remember, discipline was part of your schooling; although, it must be said, some teachers, sometimes, went a mite too far.

Today, we live in an age of crave. A craving for money, possessions and drugs. Criminals will steal, use violence, and sometimes even kill, to acquire them.

Once, back in another age, in a time that is now just a memory, things were different. Old people were respected and revered. Why? Because they were hard-working, honest and decent folk, who had overcome the trials of poverty and hardship, and were still with us to tell the tale; because, let's face it, old folk and their memories, are without a doubt, the history of life itself.

"DO YOU REMEMBER?"